Exploring the Seasons
Exploring Spring

by Terri DeGezelle

CAPSTONE PRESS
a capstone imprint

Pebble Plus is published by Capstone Press,
1710 Roe Crest Drive, North Mankato, Minnesota 56003.
www.capstonepub.com

Library of Congress Cataloging-in-Publication Data
DeGezelle, Terri, 1955–
   Exploring spring / by Terri DeGezelle.
      p. cm. — (Pebble plus. Exploring the seasons)
   Includes bibliographical references and index.
   Summary: "Color photos and simple text introduce the spring season"—Provided by publisher.
   ISBN 978-1-4296-7697-7 (library binding) — ISBN 978-1-4296-7910-7 (paperback)
   1. Spring—Juvenile literature. I. Title. II. Series.
   QB637.5.D438 2012
   508.2—dc23   2011029890

Editorial Credits

Gillia Olson, editor; Sarah Bennett, designer; Svetlana Zhurkin, media researcher; Kathy McColley, production specialist

Photo Credits

Capstone Studio: Karon Dubke, cover (center); Shutterstock: 1000 Words, 16–17, Andreas Gradin, 19, Blaz Kure, 20
(inset), Dawid Zagorski, 20–21, Glenda M. Powers, 4–5, Jeanne Hatch, 1, Sviecia, 12–13, Tony Zelenoff, cover (right);
Svetlana Zhurkin, 11, 14–15

Note to Parents and Teachers

The Exploring the Seasons series supports national science standards related to earth science.
This book describes and illustrates the spring season. The images support early readers in
understanding the text. The repetition of words and phrases helps early readers learn new
words. This book also introduces early readers to subject-specific vocabulary words, which are
defined in the Glossary section. Early readers may need assistance to read some words and to
use the Table of Contents, Glossary, Read More, Internet Sites, and Index sections of the book.

Printed in the United States of America in North Mankato, Minnesota.
102011   006405CGS12

Table of Contents

New Life

Spring is the season of new life.

Animals have babies.

Flowers grow. In the Northern

Hemisphere, the first day of

spring is March 20 or 21.

Changing Seasons

Earth spins on a tilted axis

as it goes around the sun.

Earth's tilt makes different parts

of the planet point at the sun

at different times of the year.

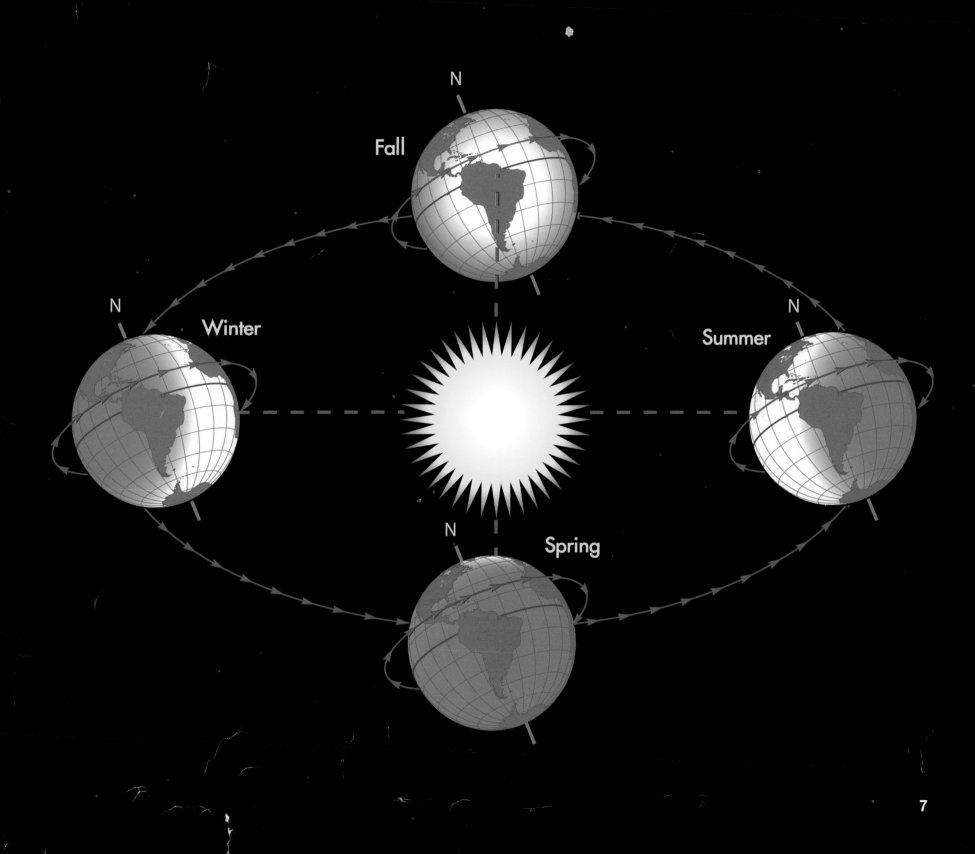

Fall

Winter

Summer

Spring

The seasons change as different parts of Earth point at the sun. Spring begins as Earth's axis just begins to point toward the sun.

Daylight

In spring the sun is higher

in the sky than in winter.

Daylight lasts longer.

Temperatures start to rise,

and the air begins to warm.

Water in Spring

Winter snow and ice start
to melt in the warm weather.
Spring rain falls instead of snow.
The wet ground is ready
for new plants to grow.

Trees in Spring

In spring, sap flows inside tree trunks again. People tap maple trees for sap to make syrup. Tree buds open into leaves and flowers.

Animals in Spring

Spring brings animal activity.

Bears come out of hibernation.

Birds return from their winter

homes and make nests.

Baby animals are born.

People in Spring

After a cold winter, people
are ready to be outdoors.
Winter coats are put away and
raincoats come out. Soccer and
baseball practices begin.

North and South

Spring in the Northern Hemisphere is fall in the Southern Hemisphere. As U.S. farmers plant crops in spring, Australian farmers harvest fall crops.

Glossary

axis—a real or imaginary line through an object's center, around which the object turns

bud—a small shoot on a plant that grows into a leaf or a flower

harvest—to gather crops that are ripe

hemisphere—one half of Earth; the Northern and Southern hemispheres experience seasons opposite to each other

hibernation—a long winter sleep of some animals in cold climates

sap—a sticky, watery fluid that flows inside plants and trees

season—one of the four parts of the year; winter, spring, summer, and fall are seasons

temperature—how hot or cold something is

tilt—leaning; not straight

Read More

Bekkering, Annalise. *Spring.* Seasons. New York: Weigl Publishers, 2011.

Emerson, Carl. *The Busy Spring.* Read-It! Readers: Science. Minneapolis: Picture Window Books, 2009.

Latta, Sara L. *Why Is It Spring?* Why Do We Have Seasons? Berkeley Heights, N.J.: Enslow Publishers, Inc., 2012.

Internet Sites

FactHound offers a safe, fun way to find Internet sites related to this book. All of the sites on FactHound have been researched by our staff.

Here's all you do:

Visit *www.facthound.com*

Type in this code: 9781429676977

Check out projects, games and lots more at **www.capstonekids.com**

Index

Word Count: 225

Grade: 1

Early-Intervention Level: 21

24